MW01054077

coffee

Jane Pettigrew

CHARTWELL
BOOKS, INC.

This edition published in 1999 by
CHARTWELL BOOKS, INC.
A division of BOOK SALES, INC
114 Northfield Avenue,
Edison, New Jersey 08837

Produced by
PRC Publishing Ltd,
Kiln House, 210 New Kings Road, London SW6 4NZ

© 1999 PRC Publishing Ltd.

ISBN 0 78581 058 7

Printed and bound in Hong Kong

Contents

Introduction

A GOLDEN LIQUOR

"Coffee is the common man's gold, and like gold, it brings to every man the feeling of luxury and nobility. Where coffee is served, there is grace and splendor and friendship and happiness. All cares vanish as the coffee cup is raised to the lips." Those words of Sheikh Abd-al-Kadir, written in 1587, express the sentiments of many thousands of coffee drinkers around the world.

All the popular stories about the origins of coffee tell how, some time in the 3rd century AD, a quiet and responsible Abyssinian goatherd by the name of Kaldi became anxious one night when his goats did not return to the fold. When he went off to look for them he found them dancing and prancing on their hind legs close to a shrub whose berries they had been munching and which had obviously given them a strange energy that Kaldi had never seen in them before. He is said to have tasted the berries for himself and found that they filled him with energy too, just as they had the goats. Kaldi's wife apparently encouraged him to take this wonderful "gift from heaven" to the local monastery, but the Abbot's reactions were not favorable and he flung the berries into the fire, discarding them as "devil's work." The aroma given off by the berries roasting in the flames brought all the other monks rushing to find out what was causing the wonderful smell and the coffee beans were raked from the ashes and gathered up. The Abbot changed his mind, suggested that the beans should be soaked in water to see what kind of a brew they gave, and the monks soon discovered that the brew kept them awake during prayers and periods of meditation. News of the wonderful powers of the drink spread from

monastery to monastery and so gradually to the wider world.

Another legend tells how Sheikh Omar was banished to the mountains for misdemeanors at court and had to live in the wild. In his experiments with different fruits and berries, he discovered that coffee cherries were helpful in curing certain ailments and so when he returned from exile with some beans from which to grow this wonderful new plant, he was made patron saint of coffee growers.

BEYOND ETHIOPIA

Botanical evidence suggests that the coffee plant originates from central Ethiopia (where it still grows wild several thousand feet above sea level). Nobody seems to know exactly when the first coffee was drunk there (or indeed anywhere), but records tell of it being drunk in its native land in the middle of the 15th century. We also know that it was cultivated in the Yemen (formerly known as Arabia) with government approval round about the same time and it is thought that perhaps the Persians had brought it here as early as the 6th century AD during their invasions of the region.

As coffee became more and more popular, special rooms in wealthier houses were set aside for coffee drinking, and coffee houses began to appear in the cities. The first opened in Mecca during the late 1400s and early 1500s and although these were originally places of religious gatherings, these large halls where customers sat on straw mats or cushions on the floor quickly became centers for music, dancing, singing, chess games, backgammon, conversation, and business dealings. Their popularity spread to Cairo, Constantinople, and beyond to all parts of the Middle East, but devout Muslims disapproved of all intoxicating beverages, including coffee, and saw the coffee houses as a threat to religious observance. At times, these popular centers of relaxation were attacked and damaged by religious fanatics, and some rulers and governments backed the prohibition of coffee drinking with dreadful punishments such as beatings and being thrown into the Bosphorous, sewn inside a leather bag.

c o f f e e

TO THE REST OF THE WORLD

By the time the Ottoman Grand Vizir Koprili was passing these stringent laws in 1656, people in other continents were learning of the pleasures of the new drink and enjoying it in their own coffee houses.

Although the Arabs tried to stop coffee seeds from being taken out of the region, inevitably travelers and merchants managed to carry some with them and the plant was cultivated in India and, some say, also in Ceylon in the early 16th or early 17th century. A Muslim pilgrim by the name of Baba Budan is said to have taped some seeds to his stomach in order to smuggle them out of Arabia and into southern India where he planted them and established the first Indian plantation.

Meanwhile, European traders from Holland, Germany, and Italy were certainly exporting beans and also trying to introduce the crop to their colonies. The Dutch were the first to start commercial cultivation in Ceylon in 1658, then in Java in 1699, and by 1706 they were exporting the first Java coffee and extending production into other parts of Indonesia. In 1714, the successful Dutch presented Louis XIV of France with a coffee tree which he grew in a glasshouse at Versailles and when this bore fruit, seeds were propagated and plants taken for cultivation to the island of Réunion, at that time called the Island of Bourbon. The variety of coffee bush that developed from that tree in Paris became known as the Bourbon coffee plant and was the original source for beans that are today grown in Brazil as Santos and in Mexico as Oxaca.

Gradually, over the next 100 years or so, plantations were established in various parts of South America, in Jamaica, in Central America, and later in Africa. And so the drink that the Arabs called "qahwah" and which was first used to keep them awake during religious meditations had found its way as a pleasurable beverage to all other parts of the world.

COFFEE DRINKING AROUND THE WORLD

In Ethiopia, coffee was originally used as a food. The ground beans were mixed with animal fat and shaped into small balls. The fat gave energy and the coffee kept travelers awake on long journeys. Today, the drink is still brewed

Top: Heated debate at the Turk's Head coffee house in London, 1770.

Center: Interior of a Turkish coffee house in 1854.

Above: Iced coffee is popular in warm climates.

with a ceremony that indicates the local respect for its history and origins.

In Yemen, the national beverage is still brewed from the coffee cherries or "Qishr" (rather than the beans) which are mixed with cinnamon, cardamom, cloves, or ginger. For holidays and special occasions, coffee beans are roasted and brewed then served with foods such as dried fruits, toasted corn kernels, nuts, and a kind of shortcake.

In the Middle East the beans are roasted very dark and ground almost to a powder, then boiled up in an "ibrik" (in various countries also known kanika, tanaka, briki) with sugar and spices (see page 34). The drink is still the symbol of hospitality. At home, it is brewed and offered to guests as soon they arrive — the eldest and most respected visitor always being given the first small syrupy cup of frothed "Turkish" coffee. It is a typical irony of life that this type of coffee is brewed in Greece, Egypt, and the Middle East, but not in Turkey! For poorer families in the Arab countries, the coffee bean itself represents wealth and success and even when there is not enough money to brew coffee every day, the beverage always holds a central placc in celebrations and special occasions.

In Greece, the tradition has always been to drink tiny cupfuls of Turkish style coffee, or maybe an espresso, with an accompanying glass of iced water, but the modern trend, especially in very hot weather is for Nescafé Frappe — a blended frothy mix of soluble coffee powder, ice, milk, and sugar — drunk from a tall glass through a straw. Apparently the mixture was "invented" in 1956, the idea spread slowly, and now everyone is drinking it.

In 17th century Turkey, European visitors reported that the locals enjoyed a drink of black color which they drank in long draughts as a kind of dainty and sipped slowly while talking with friends. Today, business is often done over a cup of coffee and Turkish coffee houses play an important role in the social life of the country.

In the Sudan, beans are dark roasted over charcoal, ground with cloves and other spices and then steeped in a jug before being strained into small cups.

In Cuba, they drink their coffee dark, rich and very sweet. The day starts for most people with several cups of espresso with condensed

Top: Florians coffee shop in Venice has been renowned for centuries. The poet Lord Byron was once a frequent customer.

Above: A typical pavement café in Paris.

milk (fresh milk is rationed to those families with children, so powdered and tinned milk is used by most people), then later in the day espresso without milk is preferred. Whatever kind of coffee Cubans drink, it is always syrupy sweet.

In southern India, coffee is the first drink of the morning and more is consumed throughout the day. It is mixed with palm sugar and milk and served with spicy sweet and savoury nibbles made from favorite ingredients such as lentils, potatoes, semolina, rice, coconut, coriander, onions, and mustard.

It was the Italians who were the first to import coffee to Europe but the market did not have an auspicious start. The catholic priests tried to have it banned as the drink of infidels, but Pope Clement VIII (1592-1605) — a gentle, thoughtful man who apparently never took hasty decisions — decided to try the new beverage for himself. He liked it and declared that Italy could not simply leave this delicious brew to the followers of Satan but should be accepted as a true Christian drink. It became particularly popular in Venice where the city's most famous coffee house, Florians, was opened in 1720 in the Piazza San Marco. From that date onwards, "caffes" were established all over Italy. Today, the Italians (and other southern Europeans) take their coffee very seriously, drinking intensely strong and rich espressos from little china cups at any time of the day.

The first Parisian coffee house opened in 1668 and, although tea was fashionable for a time in France, coffee quickly became the most popular national drink. By 1800, there were approximately 3,000 cafés in Paris. Today, the French morning cup of strong coffee mixed with plenty of hot milk is drunk from a large bowl or cup, while in the evening a smaller cup of black coffee is the preferred after dinner drink.

The Finns are the world's leading coffee drinking nation and prefer their coffee strong and black. Per capita consumption in Finland is 23.1lb (10.5kg) of roasted coffee per year. Some people say this is due to the very cold climate, others explain that in the past alcohol was rarely drunk and instead coffee and cake was served.

Sweden and Holland serve medium roast coffee with cream, while in Germany, where

Top: A group of 19th century Yemeni coffee merchants set up camp in the desert.

Above: Coffee cherries.

coffee was introduced in 1675 and has enjoyed great popularity since the beginning of the 18th century, condensed milk or tinned cream is sometimes added to the cup. In Vienna, the famous coffee houses serve deliciously rich cakes and pastries to accompany coffee with whipped cream. In Russia, black coffee is served with sugar and a slice of lemon.

In England, the city of Oxford was the first to offer its public a coffee house in 1650 and London's first opened in the Cornhill in the city in 1652. These male-dominated establishments served alcohol as well as tea, chocolate, and coffee, but it was tea that gradually took over as the most important of the three. In the 1950s, coffee bars were all the rage in London and the big cities, overshadowing tea's importance for a while — but it was a craze which did not last. However, the late 1990s are seeing something of a renaissance, with coffee bars opening in every shopping street and mall all over Britain and a better quality cup of coffee becoming more generally available. But, although the British are demonstrating a greater respect for a "good" cup of coffee, they still shy away from straight espressos and show instead a preference for milkier cappuccinos and lattes.

The newly settled immigrants to North America became coffee drinkers almost as soon as the first stocks were being shipped by the Dutch in the middle of the 17th century. Boston's first coffee retail store opened in 1650 and the first coffee house in the same city was established in 1689. And by the time the British took New Amsterdam from the Netherlands in 1664 and renamed it New York, coffee houses were opening all over the city and in other major towns. During the Mexican American War and the Civil War, coffee was always amongst the daily rations handed out to the soldiers and was brewed every evening around the campfires. Pioneers, cowboys, settlers, and explorers all made sure that they carried some coffee beans with them when they traveled west. Since the 1970s, America has shown a growing interest in quality roast and ground coffees and the new and growing coffee bar culture has changed the face of American cities and the style in which the beverage is brewed and drunk.

Top: Coffee, fancy cakes, and pastries are served at a Viennese coffee house.

Center: An American coffee bar in the 1950s.

Above: American cowboys drinking coffee.

WHAT IS COFFEE?

Although there are about 25 different varieties of the coffee plant, only two are grown for commercial coffee production. *Coffea arabica* is a large bush that originates from Ethiopia and flourishes at high altitudes above 2,000ft (600m) above sea level. Its leaves are dark green and oval and the oval fruits (the coffee cherries) contain two seeds or beans that give the best quality coffee. It was first cultivated in Yemen at the southern tip of the Arabian Peninsular and still grows wild in Ethiopia. *Coffea robusta* is a small tree which originates in the Congo and thrives below 2,000ft (600m). The round fruits contain smaller oval beans that give a poorer quality coffee with a harsher flavor. One of *robusta*'s main advantages is its resistance to disease.

Coffees from many different producing countries around the world all have their own flavors and characteristics and the reasons for this are the differences of climate (rainfall, amount of sunshine, temperature, humidity, winds, seasonal changes, etc.), elevation, plant varieties, soil types, and soil contents in the growing areas. As grapes produce thousands of different wines, and the tea plant gives us more than 3,000 different types of tea, so the coffee plant creates a widely differing spectrum of flavors and aromas depending on local variations in natural phenomena.

All varieties of the coffee plant like warmth and humidity and thrive in the well-watered regions of tropical countries in the equatorial belt that runs from 25°N to 30°S. They like generous amounts of rain and steady temperatures close to 70°F (21°C), and grow well in the heat and humidity of African forests, on Brazil's vast southern plains or on the high slopes of South American mountains where the air is cooler and damp. The bushes prefer rich volcanic soil, need good drainage and plenty of shade so that the fruit is protected from direct strong sunshine. *Arabica* trees like a temperate climate, while *robusta* prefers equatorial heat and humidity, and both types of plant will die in very cold conditions.

The bushes are usually grown in nurseries from seeds that have been carefully selected from bushes that produce the best flavor, the best crop, and are most resistant to disease.

After a few months, when the new plants are several inches high, they are transferred to pots or bags and then, when they are one year old and about 1½-2ft tall, they are transplanted to the plantation or smallholding. After three or four years, they start bearing fruit and can go on producing for up to 40 years, although they are at their best at 10-15 years. If left to grow naturally, the bushes would grow up to 30ft (9m) tall, but they are pruned regularly to a height of about six feet.

The coffee plant's cherry-like fruits develop from the delicate sweet-smelling flowers that blossom in clusters along the branches. The berries are green at first, then yellow and finally they ripen to a rich crimson red. When they are really dark red, they are ready for harvesting. Because of the even climate in many of the growing regions, bushes often bear flowers, green beans, and red beans at the same time.

Beneath the outer skin there is a fleshy fruit. Under that is a membrane that protects the bean from the cherry's soft pulp, and beneath that a "parchment" layer, inside which are two flat-faced beans that fit closely together. *Arabica* bushes generally take six to eight months for their fruit to ripen, while *robusta* cherries are ready to pick nine to eleven months after flowering.

In most growing areas, there is one coffee harvest each year, but in some countries where the climate remains fairly constant throughout the year, the bushes produce two crops. In some countries, particularly in areas close to the equator and where plantations lie at differing elevations, the fruit can be gathered right through the year.

One bush gives approximately 12lb (2.7kg) of cherries each year which yield 4-5lb (0.9-1.1kg) of beans.

HARVESTING THE CROP

The harvest takes place at different times in different producing regions. In countries that lie to the south of the equator, the crop is gathered from April to July or August. In areas north of the equator, the harvest goes on from September to December.

Choosing the exact time to harvest is crucial. If the cherries are under-ripe, the beans will not be fully developed or ripened inside and will not ripen after picking. If the fruit is over-ripe, the beans will be spoilt, and just one bad bean in a sack or a hopper can taint the rest and give a sour or bitter taste. As the cherries ripen at different speeds, the best method of harvesting is for the pickers to only gather a few at a time and then keep going back to the same bushes, every ten days or so, until the entire crop has been harvested. Although this type of selective picking is obviously expensive because of labor charges, it is the method employed in the majority of producing regions.

The alternative is strip picking when the entire crop is gathered all in one go by hand or machine. It is only viable to use mechanical harvesters on flat land where trees have been planted in regular straight lines. The harvesters pass between the rows of trees and shake the ripe cherries into hoppers. This means that there is always a certain amount of over-ripe and under-ripe cherries, twigs, and leaves mixed in with the fruits and these have to be removed before the cherries are processed. In some places everything is stripped off the trees including leaves, flowers, and cherries, and the bushes can take up to two years to recover. This kind of strip picking always results in an inferior quality coffee.

A picker can gather between 100lb (22.5kg) and 200 lb (45kg) of cherries a day, but this only yields between 20lb (4.5kg) and 40 lb (9kg) of actual beans.

PROCESSING THE BEANS

Once the fruits have been gathered, they are processed by one of two methods. The "dry" method is used for lower quality beans where there is plenty of predictable sunshine, and is the cheapest and easiest of the two. The "wet" method is more expensive, more complicated and requires large volumes of water, but it produces better quality coffee.

Separating bean from cherry

By the "dry" method, the cherries are spread out in the sunshine for three to four weeks and raked from time to time to turn them over, to ensure even drying and avoid any fermentation that would occur if moisture was trapped under or between the fruits. The outer pulp loses its water content and becomes brittle and can then be hulled away from the bean. The

Top: Coffee cherries on the branch.

Center: Workers picking the cherries in Colombia.

Above: Beans are spread in the sunshine to dry.

beans processed in this way are referred to as "naturals." In some areas, where predictable sunshine for drying cannot be assured, the pulp is stripped from the beans before sun-drying in order to shorten the process.

When the "wet" method is used, the flesh of the cherry is mechanically stripped from the beans as soon as possible after harvesting and then the beans are soaked in water for 12-36 hours during which time they begin to ferment. This loosens the inner skin which can then be washed away.

In Brazil, beans are sometimes "semi-washed" by a process that involves a much shorter fermentation time and leaves more flavor and character in beans that perhaps would otherwise lack personality.

Drying, Milling, and Polishing the Beans

Once the beans have been removed from the cherries by either of the two methods, they are still coated in a very thin layer of "parchment" which must also be given a chance to dry so that the bean can be stored successfully in a stable condition. So the beans are spread out in the sun for about 14 days, or they are laid out on trays or tables and dried by mechanical dryers. During this part of the process, they are turned regularly to make sure that they dry evenly. After this stage, they are called "parchment coffee" and can be stored for up to a year.

Just before being exported, the parchment is removed by hulling machines and then any remaining fine layers are removed by polishing machines that give the beans an attractive, shiny appearance and a bluish color.

Different types of bean

The different varieties of coffee bush all produce beans of a fairly standard size and shape, but there are a few exceptions.

Peaberry beans

Sometimes, only one seed forms inside the coffee cherry and the single bean, because there is no restriction to its development from a second seed, is round rather than flat on one side and convex on the other. Because it takes all the goodness from the cherry's flesh and doesn't have to share it with a twin bean, it gives a more concentrated flavor and, because of its regular shape, a more even roast. Peaberries are also known as "male berries" or "caracol."

Top: Operating a mechanical depulping machine —
Ivory Coast.

Above: Beans are laid out on tables to dry.

Elephant beans

Officially called the Maragogype after the area of Brazil where they were first identified, elephant beans are twice the size of normal beans. The best Maragogypes today come from Guatemala, Mexico, and Nicaragua.

Elephant Ears

These develop when one of the seeds inside the cherry grows around the other. So when they fall apart during processing, both beans have one concave side (instead of flat) and one curved side.

Sorting and Grading

After the various stages of the process, the beans are graded according to size and shape by being passed through a series of grading screens that have holes of varying sizes. They are then further graded by weight and are finally picked over, usually by hand, as they pass along a conveyor belt, to remove any beans of different sizes such as peaberries, damaged beans, stones, and debris.

Grading terminology is different in each producing country. In Colombia, the best beans are called "supremo" and the lowest grade is "pasilla" and is not good enough to be exported. Colombian producers often throw together the best two grades — "supremo" and "extra" — with a mix of peaberries of both those grades to make what they call "excelso."

In Kenya, an ABC system is used, with AA being the very best.

In Costa Rica, the top grade is "Strictly Hard Bean" and varies down through "Good Hard Bean," "Hard Bean," "Medium Hard Bean," with other names depending on the growing region — "High Grown Atlantic," "Medium Grown Atlantic," and "Low Grown Atlantic."

After grading, the beans are packed into sacks and stored until needed for export. Samples are sent to brokers who roast, taste, and assess individual types of coffee before deciding what to buy.

Most coffee companies around the world prefer to buy unroasted beans from the producers, or roasted beans from a roasting company in the country where they are to be bought by the consumer. This means that the beans can be stored for longer and it gives roasters, blenders, and packers more control over roasting standards and temperatures.

Top: Workers in Indonesia busy sorting the beans.

Center: A modern automatic sorting machine.

Above: Beans in sacks ready to ship.

COFFEE CLASSIFICATIONS

Because there are so many different varieties of the coffee plant that produce beans with differing flavors, characteristics, and styles, all of which can be prepared by a variety of methods, professionals have devised a system of assessing the quality and flavor.

Different producing countries use different systems to classify their coffees, but four general classifications are used:

"High grown milds" refers to coffees grown over 2,000ft (600m) above sea level, and usually between 4,000-6,000ft (1,200-1,800m).

"Brazils" — a term used for all *arabica* beans produced in Brazil at altitudes lower than 2,000ft (600m).

"Milds" — used to describe low grown *arabica* beans from countries other than Brazil.

"Robustas" — *robusta* beans produced mainly in Africa, Brazil, and southeast Asia.

Further classifications are made according to:
• variety of plant
• method of processing (e.g. washed, dry method)
• altitude at which the crop was grown
• size of the bean (elephant, peaberry, etc.)
• age of the beans (most green beans improve with age while some lose their quality)
• name of the plantation where the crop was grown or the area of production (Colombian, Java, etc.)

When the beans reach the professional tasters, yet more criteria are applied to evaluate individual coffees. First the tasters examine the unroasted green bean. Then they look carefully at the ground freshly roasted coffee. Then the grounds are infused in water and immediately smelled. After infusing for a further three minutes, the liquor is smelled again. Any scum on the top of the brew is then removed and the coffee is tasted. The tasters slurp, taste, and spit, and an assessment is made according to the type of bean, the appearance, and smell of both the green and the roasted bean, the aroma, the taste, the body, the acidity, the fullness of flavor, any defects, and the general drinking qualities.

Top: Jamaica's Blue Mountains.

Above: Coffee tasters are highly experienced.

What do the Tasters Mean?

The following terms are constantly used to define the qualities of individual coffees. They help coffee tasters to assess the beans' quality and character, and coffee merchants to guide their customers towards the coffees that best suit personal preferences.

Acidity — is what gives the coffee its "brightness," the pleasant tartness, snap, or dryness that the coffee leaves at the back of the palate and around the edges of the tongue; coffees with low acidity are usually smooth in the mouth; those with high acidity give a fresh, clean brew; an acidy taste can sometimes become a little winey — a quality that is very evident in Ethiopian coffees.

Flavor — can vary from light, fragrant, and mild to intense, spicy, and rich; flavors depend on the aroma, body, and acidity of the beans.

Body — describes the way the coffee feels in the mouth, the texture and creaminess, whether it has a heaviness, richness, or thickness on the back of the tongue — for example, Ethiopian mocha is light, whereas Sumatran coffee is heavy, and Brazilian Santos is somewhere between the two.

Aroma — refers to the characteristic smell of an individual coffee and can range from sweet and fragrant or delicately nutty to chocolatey, smoky, spicey, hints of burnt caramel, etc.

SPECIALTY AND BLENDED COFFEES

Unblended coffees are known as single source, specialty, original, straight, or unblended coffees. Blended coffees can be a mix of beans from different regions or estates in one country, or a mix of beans from different producing countries around the world.

In many of the producing countries, coffee is grown by smallholder farmers who sell their processed beans to a broker or exporter. It is therefore unusual to find coffees available on the market that come from a named estate or plantation, although some do exist — for example Papua New Guinea Arona Valley. Most specialty coffees are a blend of beans from a particular area or country — for example, Nicaragua, Costa Rica, etc.

24

There are two reasons for blending coffees. One is to produce a coffee that is better and more complete in flavor, body, acidity, and aroma than a straight, unblended coffee. The other is to cut costs by mixing the more expensive beans with cheaper, lower quality types. Blends are also made up to give the consumer a choice of strengths and flavors — for example, an Italian roast with a dark heavy taste, a breakfast blend with a strong, aggressive flavor and effect, or an espresso blend to give just the right intensity and a hint of burnt caramel. Each packer and blender creates its own special blends to suit customers' requirements and expectations. These blends are made up of a number of coffees of differing qualities and flavors that have been carefully selected from all those available from around the world.

ROASTING THE BEANS

Whereas the flavor and quality of a blend is predicted by the mixture of beans, the strength is determined by the roast. This can vary from a light or pale roast which gives a mild gentle brew, through medium, full, double, or high roast which gives a really strong black coffee that is ideal for making espresso. In France and Spain, a little sugar is sometimes added to give the beans a shiny caramelised coating. Italian roasters sometimes also add a little butter and this enhances the shiny oily appearance. Different roasts suit different beans from different growing regions — for example, a medium roast best suits beans from Jamaica as it brings out the full fruity flavor, but a high roast is better to develop the richness and depth of Mexican or Nicaraguan beans.

The green beans are roasted in order to develop the flavor and body and the roasting is a very skilled part of the process. During the roasting — which for the greater part of the process is normally carried out at temperatures of approximately 390-425°F (200-220°C) — 20% of the water content is evaporated and chemical changes take place that convert starch to sugar, develop soluble oils, and release gases from inside the bean. Roast for too short a time and the beans will taste flat and dull, too long and the coffee will be burnt or bitter. It is also very important that the beans are kept moving during the roasting process so that they can cook evenly.

coffee

Although green beans will keep for months or even years if stored carefully in airtight packs, roasted beans do not keep well and most roasting companies prefer to roast daily in response to customers' orders.

It is essential to protect roasted beans from oxygen, light, heat, and moisture, so more and more companies vacuum pack their product into foil or laminate bags. A recent development is the valve bag that allows carbon dioxide given off by the beans after roasting to escape but prevents other gases from entering the bag.

Naming the Roast

Different roasters and different countries have different terms for the level of roast. The following are some of the most commonly used:

Appearance of beans	Name of roast	What happens to the beans
The lightest beans	light, pale, cinnamon New England, half city	The body and and subtlety not developed; still tastes "green"
Medium brown	medium, regular, medium high, brown, British, American	High acidity, more flavor beginning to develop
Chestnut color	high, special, city, full city	Full character, sugars and acids evenly developed
Dark brown, oily surface	dark, continental, after dinner, espresso, double, high roast	Natural oils brought to the surface; flavor becomes sweeter and smoother
Very dark, almost black shiny surface	black, heavy, French, Belgian, Italian	Strong pungent flavor develops

Top: Green coffee beans.

Center: The traditional way to roast beans in Indonesia.

Above: The finished product, roasted coffee beans.

FLAVORED COFFEES

In the Middle East, cardamom and cinnamon have traditionally been added to coffee for centuries and today the newer trend for more exotic flavored coffees that started in America has spread to Europe and elsewhere over the last few years. To produce the very wide range that is now available, roasted beans are sprayed with oils that carry the flavorings for such varieties as chocolate fudge, butter crunch, raspberry cream, streussel cake, vanilla nut cream, Hawaiian hazelnut, sticky toffee pudding, etc.

If grinding flavored beans at home, it is important to be aware that the grounds may well taint any beans that are subsequently ground in the same machine.

Flavored brewed coffees are now also offered on the menus of coffee bars, made with shots of espresso, hot milk and syrups flavored with such things as caramel, amaretto, Irish cream, or French vanilla.

DECAFFEINATED COFFEE

Most decaffeinated coffees are processed in Germany or Switzerland. Three methods are used to remove caffeine from green beans. The most common today is the Swiss Water Process which involves soaking the beans in water and filtering the caffeine through a carbon filter. This method also removes all the flavor from the beans so the water that has been used for soaking is evaporated to distil the flavors which are then sprayed back onto the beans after they have been dried.

An alternative method is to steam the beans until they expand and open, then remove the caffeine with the solvent methylene chloride which does not remove all the flavors along with the caffeine.

For those coffee drinkers who wish to cut down on caffeine intake, it is possible to choose your beans accordingly. High roasts contain less caffeine than medium or light roasted coffees, and *arabica* and high grown beans also contain less caffeine than *robustas*.

ORGANIC COFFEE

The growing interest in organic products, including coffee, originates in a wide concern

Top: Cardomom is mixed with the roasted beans to give a unique and very aromatic flavor.

Above: Grinding the traditional way in Indonesia.

amongst the consuming public for systems of agriculture that respect the environment, human health, and the general health of the planet. The expanding range of organic products in supermarkets, publicity, and pro-motional campaigns by organic companies, and governmental regulations have led to greater awareness.

Before any product can be marketed as organic, it must go through a rigid certification programme that checks all stages of produc-tion and manufacture from the coffee plant through to the cup to make absolutely sure that no chemical fertilizers, herbicides, fungi-cides, or insecticides are used at any stage of the process. Organic coffees are now being produced in Brazil, Venezuela, Africa, Ecuador, the Dominican Republic, Peru, Mexico, Guatemala, El Salvador, Nicaragua, Costa Rica, Sumatra, Papua New Guinea, Colombia, and Timor.

Like all organic foods, organic coffees are more expensive because their production is far more labor intensive and they are not general-ly produced on a large scale.

BUYING AND STORING COFFEE

Although it is possible to roast beans at home, it is much more satisfactory to buy beans that have been professionally roasted. And because coffee is difficult to store successfully for any length of time, it is better to buy small quantities and use as quickly as possible after purchase.

Deciding what to buy depends on personal taste and preferences for different times of the day and different occasions. The best way to decide what you really like is to try different blends and different roasts until you find what suits. Choose a supplier (either a local retailer or a mail order supplier) who can give plenty of information about origin and flavor of the products, who offers advice about grinding and brewing, and who is reliable in terms of supply, quality, consistency of flavor in blends, etc.

Once a pack of coffee beans has been opened, store it very carefully in an airtight container in a cool, dry place away from other strong-smelling foods because, like tea, coffee absorbs other flavors very easily. In an unopened vacuum bag, the beans will keep well for up to a year. In air-tight containers,

Top: Coffee beans in a shop window in Italy.

Above: Vacuum packing is an excellent way to preserve the coffee's freshness.

beans will keep in the freezer for up to a month. Do not defrost before use — grind and use from frozen. The fridge is not a good place for storage of coffee because any condensation and resulting moisture can affect the beans. Once the coffee has been ground, it will only keep for about two weeks in an airtight container because it quickly loses its essential oils and therefore its flavor. It is much better to grind the beans immediately before brewing.

THE RIGHT GRIND

Different methods of brewing and different styles of brewing equipment demand different sizes of coffee ground. The normal categorizations are fine, medium, and coarse, and the general rule is the finer the grind, the quicker the infusion, so smaller grounds do not need to be in the water for as long as larger grounds.

General Guidelines

Brewing method	Recommended Grind
Ibriq	powdered
(Turkish coffee pot)	
Espresso	very fine
Stove-top Espresso	fairly fine
Drip filter	medium
Coffee sock	medium
Plunger pot	medium
Cafetière	medium
Jug	coarse

What Sort of Grinder?

The old-fashioned hand-turned grinders are probably the best but it is important to use a good quality one in order to achieve a regular grind. The simplest to use are the electric choppers with blades or plates that crush the beans and these are available in various standards of sophistication. The most complex have individual settings for different grinds, the simplest offer less control. To achieve a grind that resembles that produced by the professionals, get a sample of the correct size of ground for your brewing machine from your retailer and use as a guideline.

Whichever type of grinder you use, always grind the beans just before brewing. Once the beans have been ground and come into contact with the air, they will immediately start to lose their essential oils, aroma, and flavor.

Top: A wooden coffee grinder.

Above: A modern electric equivalent.

coffee

Clean and dry your grinder carefully. The stale grounds will turn sour and can taint the beans you grind at a later date.

Most coffee companies today sell a "multi-purpose" grind and mark the packet "Suitable for all coffee makers." This can lead to problems. If a fine espresso grind is used in a cafetière, it will be difficult to push down the plunger because of resistance from the layer of coffee. This can lead to dangerous spillages. Using an all-purpose grind can also affect the quality of the infusion since a fine grind can easily overbrew in a system where it remains in contact with the water for too long, and the full flavor of a coarse grind will not be extracted if the coffee is infused for too short a time.

DIFFERENT BREWING METHODS

Most methods of coffee brewing demand the use of water that has been boiled and allowed to cool for a few minutes. Boiling water draws out a certain bitterness from the beans.

Ibriq (Turkish coffee pot)

Ibriqs are a small long-handled pots made of brass or copper. This method is based on the traditional Arabian way of making coffee and uses boiling water which can make the brew taste bitter. The Arabs often add spices to soften that bitterness.

To work out how many little cups of Turkish coffee they will make, measure the capacity before starting. Use medium-high roast beans that have been ground to a fine powder. For four cups of coffee, use four heaped teaspoons of powdered coffee grounds, four heaped teaspoons of sugar (or more or less to taste) and four small coffee cups of water.

Put the water and sugar into the ibriq (or a small saucepan) and bring to the boil. Remove from the heat, add the coffee, stir, and return to the heat. When the mixture bubbles up to the rim of the pot, lift off the stove and allow to settle. Put back on the heat and when the coffee boils up for the second time, pour a little of the froth on the surface into each of the cups. Boil up once more and then allow the grounds to settle before pouring into the cups.

If liked, add the crushed seeds from one cardamom pod, vanilla, or a piece of cinnamon stick to the liquid as it boils for the third time.

introduction

Top: Turkish nomads use the traditional ibriq to prepare a strong syrupy coffee made from pulverized beans.

Above: Coffee is heated in an ibriq.

Espresso Machines

There are several different types of espresso machine available today and for a machine to be effective, it must be able to generate enough steam and pressure to extract the rich flavor from the dark roast grounds by forcing boiling water and steam through them.

Follow these rules to produce a successful espresso:

Use finely ground dark roast coffee.

Use one to two level tablespoons or grounds per cup.

Tamp the grounds down in the "gruppa" so that they are packed tightly and firmly but not so tightly that water and steam cannot pass through.

Black coffee will stream from the machine first followed by a caramel colored froth called the "crema." As this starts to flow, switch off the machine to avoid making the coffee watery and thin.

To make a good cappuccino, use cold semi-skimmed homogenised milk (rather than full fat). Put the milk into a jug and place the steam nozzle of the espresso machine just under the surface of the milk. Don't use full power, and don't push the nozzle too deep into the milk. The milk should be a mass of tiny bubbles which are then spooned onto the top of the espresso coffee.

Stove-Top Espresso Pots

These pots (also known as Moka, mocha, napo-letana pots) have two chambers and a metal fil-ter which holds the coffee grounds and sits between the two. Fill the bottom chamber with the correct amount of water. Measure the cor-rect amount of fairly fine ground coffee into the filter, cover with its lid and sit in the neck of the lower chamber. Screw the top of the pot into place and bring to the boil on the stove. As the water boils it is forced through the coffee and into the top chamber ready for pouring.

The drawback of using these pots is that they can spit the coffee out of the spout as it brews.

Drip Filters

Drip filter machines are available in various forms. The simplest method is to sit a plastic conical filter in the neck of a suitable jug, place a paper filter inside, and measure in the coffee

Top: An espresso machine.

Above: Stove-top espresso pot.

grounds. Water is then poured over the grounds and allowed to slowly filter through into the jug below.

Electric filter machines ensure that the water reaches the correct temperature before hitting the grounds and provide a plate on which the jug of brewed coffee is kept hot. Never leave the coffee sitting in a jug on the hot plate for more than about 20 minutes as it will gradually develop a bitter, stale taste. For all drip filter methods, use medium ground coffee.

The Coffee Sock

This works on exactly the same principle as the drip filter and allows the easy and effective brewing of one cup or mug of roast and ground fresh coffee. Sit the nylon or muslin sock neatly in the neck of a cup or mug, measure in the medium ground coffee, pour in a small amount of water that has boiled and cooled a little just to dampen the grounds, wait for a few moments, then add the correct measure of hot water and leave to filter through into the cup.

Plunger Pot or Cafetière

This is probably the most popular method of brewing as it is an easy and extremely effective way of extracting the best flavor from the coffee. Warm the pot before use, measure in approximately five grams of medium-coarse ground coffee (roughly a rounded dessert-spoon per cup), pour on water that has boiled and been allowed to cool slightly, leave for 4-5 minutes then push the plunger carefully down to the bottom of the pot.

The Jug Method

This basic, old fashioned method of brewing demands a coarsely ground medium to high roast bean. Measure the coffee into the jug, allowing a level dessertspoon per cup, then pour on the nearly boiling water. Leave to infuse for 4-5 minutes (or longer depending on the coarseness of the grounds) then strain into warmed cups or mugs, or into a serving jug.

Top: A drip filter percolator.

Above: Plunger pot or cafetière.

IN THE CUP

Coffee menus now offer a wide range of different brews. What do all the different terms mean?

Espresso
A rich full bodied coffee made by forcing boiling water and steam through finely ground beans.

Espresso Ristretto
The machine making the espresso is switched off before the end of the process so that the coffee is more concentrated and richer in aroma and flavor.

Americano
A shot of espresso thinned with hot water.

Doppio
A double shot of espresso.

Espresso romano
A shot of espresso with a twist of lemon peel.

Cappuccino
Made with one third espresso, one third hot milk, and one third milk froth made by passing steam through the milk to create a mass of tiny bubbles.

Caffe latte
A shot of espresso topped with a glassful or mugful of steamed milk.

Espresso macchiato
A shot of espresso with a small dash of milk.

Latte macchiato
A glass or mug of hot milk with a dash of espresso.

Caffe con panna
Espresso with cold whipped cream.

Caffe Mocha
One third espresso, one third steamed milk, one third hot chocolate.

Top: Espresso coffee.

Center: Cappucino.

Above: Caffe con panna.

BREWING THE PERFECT CUP OF COFFEE

There are many different methods of brewing coffee, but there are a few golden rules to follow each time:

Buy freshly roasted beans and store them in an airtight container in a cool, dry place or in the freezer.

Grind the beans just before using.

Choose the right grind for the method being used.

When filling the kettle or brewing machine with water, use fresh cold water from the tap or filter jug (a successful brew needs oxygen).

Use equipment that is clean and dry.

Use the correct amount of coffee, following the guidelines given by equipment manufacturers and coffee retailers and according to personal taste. Don't stint and don't try to make a stronger brew by using more coffee than recommended — it's the roast that makes for strength, not the amount of coffee used.

Don't pour boiling water onto the grounds — it will make the coffee bitter. Use water that has boiled and been allowed to cool a little.

Warm the cups or mugs before pouring coffee into them.

Don't reuse grounds.

Don't reheat left-over coffee. It will taste bitter and unpleasant.

Coffees fron

coffee

Brazil

Carwardines
54/62 Clouds Hill Road
Bristol BS5 7LB
UK
Tel: (00 44) (0)117 955 0520
Fax: (00 44) (0)117 941 3068

Brazil is the world's biggest producer of coffee from some four billion coffee trees. Many of the plantations were originally planted in the 1720s with the Bourbon strain of the plant that made its way from Louis XIV's tree in Paris via the island of Réunion to Brazil. In the past much of Brazilian coffee was pleasant but not particularly special, and was more often used in blends than sold as single source. But since 1990, when the coffee industry was freed from government control, and with an increase in world coffee prices, there is a new incentive to produce quality coffees for the international market.

The best coffees come from the state of São Paolo, where young bushes produce small curly Bourbon Santos beans. As the trees age, the beans grow flatter and larger and these, known as Flat Bean Santos, are probably Brazil's best. Coffee is grown in 16 other states and the beans from each region have their own character, although most are less acidic and offer heavier body and mouthfeel than other Central and South American coffees. Among the best are those from the Cerrado region of Minas Gerais state and washed beans from Bahia in the north east. One of the problems in the southern states is frost which kills the trees and has been known to almost destroy entire plantations and send world coffee prices soaring.

Brazilian Santos

Character: A soft, smooth, mild tasting cup.

Suggested roast: Medium.

Drinking hints: Ideal for use in a domestic espresso machine.

Supplier: Founded in Bristol, UK, in 1777, Carwardines have been roasting and blending coffee for over 200 years.

coffee

Colombia

Seattle Coffee Company
5 Rossetti Studios
72 Flood Street
London SW3 5TF
UK
Tel: (00 44) (0)171 495 5531
e.mail:
GarielleShawCommunications@compuserve.com

Colombia is second in world coffee production after Brazil and grows mainly *arabicas* on three mountain ranges that run from north to south in the foothills of the Andes. The central and eastern ranges produce the best coffees — Medellin, Armenia, and Manizales (often referred to as MAMs) which take their names from the towns or cities through which they are marketed. Medellin, with its heavy body and rich flavor, is the most famous. The other two are thinner and less acidic.

The larger plantations are run by cooperatives while other smaller farms belong to family smallholders. The coffee grows well on the well-drained, rich volcanic soil and, because the beans ripen at different times in the differing climatic conditions of the mountain regions, the crop is gathered throughout the year. Shade against the intense heat is provided by banana and rubber trees.

Colombian coffee is usually described as having a rich smooth flavor and a pleasant balance of good acidity, mellow body, and attractive flavor. At its finest it is full bodied and has a slightly winey flavor. Some of the very best is said to come from around Bogotá and Bucaramanga.

Colombia Armenia

Character: The highest grade beans from the central cordilleras of Colombia give a smooth and evenly balanced coffee with mid-depth body and mild acidity.

Suggested roast: Medium.

Drinking hints: Brew as espresso or in a filter machine or cafetière. An "easy to drink" cup, suitable for all times of the day

Supplier: Seattle Coffee Company was taken over by Starbucks, the US coffee company in 1998 and the company has over 1,700 shops worldwide.

coffee

Costa Rica

Costa
Old Paradise Street
London SE11 6AX
UK
Tel: (0044) (0)171 840 2091
e.mail: gai@dial.dipex.com

Costa Rica's first plantations were established in 1779 with plants brought from Cuba and the country is today a highly respected coffee producer. Most of Costa Rica's coffee is grown on the best and most fertile land around the capital San José where the volcanic soil is well-drained, rich, and black. The yield per hectare has increased over the last 30 years and is the highest in the world, with a national average of 1.5 tons (1,524kg) per hectare.

The height at which the *arabica* trees are grown is very important for two reasons — it produces a high level of acidity in the beans, and the cooler air that surrounds the trees in the evening and at night means that the coffee cherries develop and ripen more slowly, giving the coffees a much richer, more robust flavor and a full bodied heartiness. The beans are graded as "Strictly Hard Bean" (SHB) if they have been grown above 3,900ft (1,200m) and "Good Hard Bean" from elevations between 3,300ft (1,000m) and 3,900ft. The best from this area are Tres Rios (mild and sweet with bright acidity), Tarrazu (full bodied, sweet, and powerful with excellent acidity), and Alajuela (powerfully acidic and balanced).

Costa Rica San Marco Tarrazu

Character: A mellow taste, good body, subtle acidity, and a crisp finish.

Suggested roast: Medium to high.

Drinking suggestions: Best made in a filter or plunger pot. A classic drinker, for any time of day.

Supplier: Costa has over 100 stores and coffee bars throughout the UK and has plans for more in the next two years. The company reckons that it serves two million cups of coffee a week.

coffee

Ethiopia

H R Higgins
79 Duke Street
London W1M 6AS
UK
Tel: (00 44) (0)171 629 3913
Fax: (00 44) (0)1992 787523

Ethiopia is thought to be the original source of coffee and the name is said to come from the town of Kaffa. Today, most of the coffee is produced at elevations of 5,000ft (1,500m) above sea level where there is a mixture of modern plantations, smallholder plots, and wild coffee growing on the mountain slopes. Connoisseurs say that the finest Ethiopian coffees are among their true favorites and they seek out both the washed and sundried beans that the country produces. Unwashed Harrars have an inconsistency, but at their best are fruity and spicy, full bodied, and slightly bitter. These come from the highest plantations and are classified as Shortberry or Longberry, the latter being the better of the two. Others to look out for are Sidamo, Djimmah, Lekempti, and (the rarest which is usually exported to Germany) Yirgacheffes.

Ethiopia has a rich and ancient coffee culture — a brewing ceremony which involves special utensils, artefacts, and traditions — and the people consume the largest amount of coffee in Africa. The domestic market accounts for 150,000 tons (1.5m kg) per year and almost everyone drinks at least one cup of coffee every day. Approximately 25% of the population is involved in producing coffee in nine regions.

Ethiopian Harrar Longberry

Character: This is an interesting, gamey, slightly winey coffee with a very pungent aroma.

Suggested roast: Medium.

Drinking hints: As this is a light coffee it is not recommended for espresso but is ideally suited to the Turkish method of brewing.

Supplier: H R Higgins was founded in 1942 in a sixth floor attic in London's West End. The company now has premises in Piccadilly where customers can taste as well as buy their teas and coffees.

Guatemala

Northern Tea Merchants
Crown House
193 Chatsworth Road
Chesterfield
Derbyshire S40 2BA
UK
Tel: (00 44) (0)1246 232600 or 233660
Fax: (00 44) (0)1246 555991

Guatemala has been producing coffee since 1773, when the Jesuit priests planted it there as an ornamental plant in the monastery gardens. Almost 100 years later, several planters started to grow coffee when the indigo industry collapsed. In 1960, the industry was badly disrupted by the civil war which went on until 1996, but since the signing of the peace treaty, there have been hopes of development, and coffee growers are trying to improve productivity and yields of quality coffee.

Most of the coffee is grown by small producers, mostly ethnic Maya who live along the shores of Lake Atitlan, Guatemala's biggest crater lake. Of the four volcanic regions, Atitlan's is the richest. "Strictly Hard Bean," the highest grade, is grown above 4,500ft (1,350m), "Hard Bean" between 4,000ft (1,200m) and 4,500ft. Coffees produced are classified as "washed *arabica*" and, because the plantations are located on hillsides and mountains at different altitudes, coffee types vary in body and acidity. The finest high growns have a spicy, full bodied flavor. The most famous regions are Fraijanes, Atitlan, San Marcos, Oriente, Huehuetenango, and (the best quality) Antigua and Coban — both distinctly spicy and smoky, and rich in flavor with good body and balanced acidity.

Guatemala Genuine Antigua

Character: Medium bodied coffee with a mild, rich, sweet taste and a hint of acidity.

Suggested roast: Medium roast.

Drinking hints: A very versatile all day drinker. Brew in a filter or cafetière and drink with or without milk.

Supplier: Northern Tea Merchants dates back to 1936 and is famous in the English county of Derbyshire for its shop that offers customers the chance to taste samples from a wide range of teas and coffees.

c o f f e e

Hawaii

Torz & Macatonia
The Roastery
12 Blackwall Estate
Lanrick Road
London E14 0JP
UK
Tel: (00 44) (0)171 515 7770
Fax: (00 44) (0)171 515 7779
e.mail: TorzMacatoniaCoffee@compuserve.com

Coffee is the major crop in Hawaii, where coffee has been growing since the early 1800s. The main producing area on the Big Island is Kona. There are roughly 600 farms, each approximately three acres (1.2 hectares) in size, covering a total of 2,000 acres (800 hectares). Kona production totals more than two million pounds a year of top quality hand-harvested beans. Some farmers sell freshly picked, processed beans, but there is a trend towards marketing "value-added" coffees that have been milled and roasted on the island. The Big Island also has coffee orchards at Kau and Hamakau.

Hawaii's other coffee areas lie on the smaller islands of Oahu, where beans from over 100 acres (40 hectares) of coffee trees produce washed beans, Molokai, which has 450 acres (200 hectares) of coffee growing on the banks of the Molokai Irrigation System, Kauai, where the crop from the largest coffee plantation in the US is mechanically harvested and processed, and Maui, whose largest orchard is on the slopes of the West Maui Mountain, overlooking the beaches of Kaanapali.

Hawaiian Kona Extra Fancy

Character: This coffee has a sweetness, a light bodied fruity flavor, and natural acidity that twinkles through the cup to balance the flavor and leave a clean finish.

Recommended roast: Medium roast keeps the delicate floral acidity and allows the sweet richness to come through.

Drinking hints: Brew in a cafetière or filter machine, and drink preferably without, or perhaps just a little, milk.

Supplier: Torz & Macatonia.

Torz and Macatonia supply beans unroasted (above) for home roasting as well as roasting the coffee themselves (below).

India

Torz & Macatonia
The Roastery
12 Blackwall Estate
Lanrick Road
London E14 0JP
UK
Tel: (00 44) (0)171 515 7770
Fax: (00 44) (0)171 515 7779
e.mail: TorzMacatoniaCoffee@compuserve.com

It is said that the Muslim pilgrim, Baba Budan, managed to smuggle seven coffee seeds out of Mecca in 1600 and plant them near his home in Mysore in southern India. Commercial coffee cultivation was started in that area in the early 1800s by the British and the fertile soil and tropical climate were ideally suited to the crop. Both *arabica* and *robusta* are grown in three southern states and produce coffees that are mild, velvety, and fairly acidic. Because spices are also grown on the plantations, some of the coffees have a uniquely Indian spicy aroma and flavor. Mysore is the best known region for quality, long, wide beans that give a mild body, fair acidity, and a subtle flavor.

The most sought after of India's coffees are "Monsooned Malabar" which, like old Java beans, are stored for several weeks in order to give a mature flavor that is similar to that developed naturally when coffees took several months to reach Europe and North America by ship. The modern process exposes the dried beans to the humid monsoon winds, giving them a special mellow flavor and a low acidity. The monsooned beans become available in January each year.

Monsooned Malabar

Character: A deep, full mouthfeel, powerful, spicy aroma, and little acidity. Very creamy and full bodied.

Roast: High roast.

Drinking suggestions: This is too intense to use as an espresso coffee but is excellent brewed in a cafetière or filter machine as a winter or after dinner coffee.

Supplier: Jeremy Torz & Stephen Macatonia acquired their coffee knowledge in the US before setting up in London's thriving docklands. They share a passion for quality coffees.

Jamaica

J. Martinez & Company
3230A Peachtree Road
NE Atlanta
Georgia 30305
USA
Tel: (001) 404 231 5465
Fax: (001) 404 233 6528

The British developed coffee cultivation after its introduction here in 1730. Although other West Indian islands grow coffee, Jamaica produces the most interesting and highest quality. Blue Mountain has been recognized as one of the best in the world for a number of years and today, the genuine article is rarely available as most goes straight to the Japanese who buy roughly 90% of production. Most of the rest goes to Germany, the US, and the UK.

The Blue Mountains run in a south easterly direction from the center of Jamaica towards the south eastern tip. The coffee producing region, where the highest grown coffee in the world is produced at over 7,000ft (2,100m), covers an area of approximately 15,000 acres (6,000 hectares). More coffee than could be grown on this relatively small area is marketed every year. Other areas of the island grow High Mountain Supreme and Prime Washed Jamaican. To be sure that you are buying the real thing, look out for named estates such as Wallenford. True Blue Mountain coffee is full bodied, sweet, and fruity, with an intense aroma.

Jamaican Blue Mountain

Character: A quintissential coffee of rich flavor and aroma, full body, and moderate acidity. Possesses all the characteristics of a perfectly balanced coffee.

Suggested roast: Medium or dark.

Drinking hints: Medium roast gives a good all day drinker. A dark roast is good for an after dinner coffee. Can be brewed alone as an espresso.

Supplier: For more than a hundred years, from its base in the island of Jamaica, the Martinez family has been trading coffee, honey, and spices. John Martinez, the current head of the company is the fourth generation of the family.

Java

Whittard of Chelsea
73 Northcote Road
London SW11 6PJ
UK
Tel: (00 44) (0)171 924 1888
Fax: (00 44) (0)171 924 3085

The first plantations in Java were established by the Dutch in 1699 at the suggestion of Amsterdam's burgermaster, Nicolaas Witson. Seeds from the successful plants were offered to other European countries, including France where Louis XIV's famous Bourbon tree became the source for seedlings that went to the French colonies and South and Central America.

The island's early *arabica* estates were wiped out by disease in the 1870s and were replaced with the more resistant *robusta* plants. But today, more *arabica* has again been planted. Java coffees are rich and full bodied with a strong, slightly smoky, spicy flavor.

In the past, during the long journey by ship from the island to markets in North America and Europe, the beans acquired a special maturity, and customers became so used to the more mellow flavor that they refused to accept younger more acidic beans. So Indonesian producers developed a system of storing the beans for several years in warehouses prior to export. As they age, the beans turn from pale green to brown. They are known as "go-down" or "passage" coffees and are marketed as Old Java, Aged Java, or Old Brown Java.

Old Brown Java

Character: A unique flavor quite unlike any other coffee. It has a wonderful tang and a twist of spiciness. It is full flavored with a rich and nutty, hold-on-the-tongue character.

Suggested roast: Needs a high French roast to develop its unique flavor.

Drinking suggestions: Best drunk in the evenings, with or without milk.

Supplier: Whittard of Chelsea was established in London in 1886 and now sells a wide range of teas and coffees from more than 100 shops in the UK and around the world.

coffees from around the world

coffee

Kenya

Cooper & Company
Halkett Place
St Helier
Jersey
Channel Islands UK
Tel (00 44) (0)1534 33352
Fax: (00 44) (0)1534 506879
e.mail: coopers@itl.net

Coffee arrived in Kenya from the island of Réunion in the late 1890s but the coffee industry did not really get started until the early years of the 20th century. The Germans started cultivation and the British continued it, and Kenya coffees are today among the world's best, although the country holds less than 2% of world production.

Most plantations are smallholdings in the Kenya Highlands at elevations of between 5,000ft (1,500m) and 7,000ft (2,100m). Because of temperate climatic conditions there are two crops a year. The beans are sold on to cooperatives who process and market the beans and this means that no coffees are sold by estate names only by grade names. Classifications are PB (peaberry, the single bean that grows inside one cherry instead of two), AA, AB, etc. Kenya Peaberries are among the best in the world. The coffee is sold through weekly auctions in Nairobi and the idea is that the highest quality will fetch the highest price. Over the past few years, prices have been rising, driven by consumer demand and the fact that Kenyan coffees are of consistently good quality. They have a sharp, winey flavor, and a clear, clean, intense acidity.

Kenya AA

Character: Excellent flavor and aroma with distinctive bite.

Suggested roast: Medium roast is best. a lighter roast and there's too much acidity. Roasted darker and the individuality of the coffee is lost.

Drinking hints: A good after dinner coffee, best with milk to increase smoothness. Good blended with Colombian.

Supplier: Cooper & Company is a family run business established around 1890. It is currently run by the third generation and specializes in quality teas and coffees.

It is possible to buy Cooper & Company's Kenya AA as roasted (above) or unroasted (below) beans.

Mexico

Bettys and Taylors of Harrogate
1 Parliament Street
Harrogate HG1 2QU
UK
Tel: (00 44) (0)1423 886055
Fax: (00 44) (0)1423 881083

Coffee seedlings are said to have been planted here by the Spanish in the late 18th century and today Mexico is the fourth largest producer of coffee in the world. But the beans are not generally among the world's best for, although pleasant and delicate with a dry acidity, they lack richness and body. The state of Oaxaca on the western slopes of the central highlands and Veracruz on the east grow the finest. Oaxaca State, Oaxaca Pluma, and Altura Coatepec from Vercruz are worth looking out for. These have a complex sweetness which makes them attractive as self drinkers.

American blenders have for a long time regarded Mexican coffees as good, low cost blenders and neutral fillers. Mexican producers have recently formed a trade association to promote their better quality coffees and combat the idea that the beans are inferior. Both large cooperatives and smallholder farmers are making advances in farming practices, wet processing, and milling, and quality is steadily improving. Prices are even beginning to match those of Guatemalan coffees.

Mexico is famous for its elephant beans, known as maragopypes. Supply and quality of these vary but the best give a smooth, mellow, fragrant coffee.

Mexico Maragopypes

Character: Large bean *arabica*. A light bodied coffee with fine acidity and a delicate flavor.

Suggested roast: Medium.

Drinking hints: With or without milk as an all day coffee.

Supplier: Bettys & Taylors of Harrogate was established in 1886 and sells a wide range of teas and coffees by mail order and through their five Yorkshire shops.

As well as Mexico Maragopype, Bettys and Taylors offers a range of excellent coffees.

Nicaragua

Simon Lévelt b.v
KA Hofmanweg 3
2031 BH Haarlem
HOLLAND
Tel: (00 31) 23 512214
Fax: (00 31) 23 5122505

Nicaragua has suffered over the past years from earthquakes and major political upheavals, and is the poorest country in Central America. Due to recent disasters it will probably take five to seven years for the crop to be replanted and grow to maturity. Nicaragua's agriculture accounts for roughly 30% of gross domestic product, the main exports in descending order of importance being coffee, beef, sugar, seafood, and bananas. Under the Sandanista regime, coffee growers were forced to sell through the state monopoly, but since 1991, the market has opened to competition and there are hopes of foreign investment which will help to improve the state of the industry.

The best quality *arabicas* are grown in the mountains of the north and central region of the country, and are classified as "Central Estrictamente Altura." Names to look out for are Jinotega and Matagalpa. Classifications are High Grown, Medium Grown, and Low Grown. Some blenders in the US and the UK believe that Nicaraguan coffee generally is greatly undervalued. Major customers are Western Europe, the US, and the Far East.

Nicaragua Rain Forest

Character: A mild, high grown coffee, extremely aromatic, smooth, easy to drink, and with a deep bouquet.

Suggested roast: Light to medium to maintain the fresh character.

Drinking hints: Suitable for breakfast or as an after dinner treat. Best made in a filter or plunger pot. Drink with milk.

Supplier: Simon Lévelt has been an independent family owned company for five generations since 1817 and today has 12 shops in the Netherlands.

coffee

Papua New Guinea

Espresso House
12 Viscount Court
Station Road
Brize Norton
Oxfordshire OX18 3QQ
UK
Tel: (00 44) (0)1993 851541
Fax: (00 44) (0)1993 851540

Café Liegeois SA
Route de Verviers 181
B-4651 Battice
BELGIUM
Tel: (00 31) (0)87 67 91 73
Fax: (00 31) (0)87 66 02 36

Commercial coffee production started in Papua New Guinea in the 1950s and, despite such a short history, the country is now producing some very fine coffees. The plants were cultivated from Kenya root stock and the coffees are not dissimilar from Kenyans in their strength and smoothness. Plantations are mostly smallholdings high up in the forests at elevations of 4,000ft (1,200m) to nearly 6,000ft (1,800m).

From 1975 onwards, the industry expanded rapidly, with government financial support, and unfortunately quality was sacrificed for quantity. However, a new grading system was introduced in the early 1990s and gradually, quality has returned.

Papouasie

Character: Very fine Arusha *arabica* variety from a small farm at an altitude of 5,500ft (1,650m). A well-rounded, full bodied coffee with a slightly perfumed flavor and a touch of acidity.

Drinking hints: Ground and packed to brew the perfect espresso. The coffee "pod" has been introduced by several blenders and packers for use in commercial and domestic espresso machines to ensure even and consistent brewing. Café Liegeois has taken the system one step further by producing pods containing different specialty coffees available for home consumption. The range includes Jamaica, Ethiopia, Guatemala, Kenya, Haiti, Colombia, and Java single source coffees.

Suppliers: Espresso House and Café Liegeois.

Sumatra

Peet's Tea and Coffee
PO Box 12509
Berkeley
CA 94712-3509
USA
Tel: (001) 510 594 2950
Fax: (001) 510704 0311
e.mail: webmail@peets.com

After plantations had been successfully established in Java in the late 1690s, the Dutch expanded production into Sumatra and Celebes. Indonesia was the first country to export commercially produced coffee outside Yemen. Today it is the fourth largest producer. Sumatra's estates grow mainly *arabica* on the west coast, while the eastern side of the island grows more *robusta*. The island's climate is perfectly suited to coffee production and the best crops, Mandheling and Ankola beans, are grown at 2,500 (750m) to 5,000ft (1,500m) above sea level near the port of Padang in the north western corner of the island. The natural dry milling process develops an intense concentration of flavor in the beans, and in the cup they give a syrupy sweet, smooth, and rich coffee with a wonderful flavor and aroma.

Sumatra has become famous for its Kopi Luak beans which are gathered after the small civit cats (called luaks) that live wild on the island eat the flesh from the coffee cherries but leave the beans lying on the ground.

Sumatra

Character: Very full body with concentrated flavor. Sweet, slightly earthy nuances with gutsy richness.

Suggested roast: Medium.

Drinking hints: A heavy coffee that goes well with milk, so is good for latte and cappuccino.

Supplier: When Peet's Tea and Coffee Store opened in 1966, the coffee was roasted in the shop and brewed by the cup for customers to sample. Their ideas caught on and the business grew at the vanguard of the US coffee revolution.

coffee

Tanzania

H R Higgins
79 Duke Street
London W1M 6AS
UK
Tel: (00 44) (0)171 629 3913
Fax: (00 44) (0)1992 787523

As in Kenya, coffee production was started by the Germans and taken over and developed by the British. Like other East African countries, Tanzania has plenty of land and an available labor force for the potential development of quality coffee production. Yields are still low at only 250 kg per hectare, compared to an average of one ton (1,000kg) per hectare in many Latin American and some Asian countries. Tanzania's biggest problem is in developing disease and pest-resistant varieties of the coffee plant.

Tanzania coffees are similar to Kenyans but have less acidity and body. The famous Chagga is produced by the Wa-chagga people who live and farm on the slopes of Mount Kilimanjaro. Their farms are small to medium in size and mostly belong to cooperatives. The coffees are called Kilimanjaro and Kibo (after two of the mountain's peaks), and have a well-balanced, full flavor with a delicate acidity and are much sought after by the Japanese. Others to look out for are Moshi, Mbeya, and Arusha, named after the shipping ports that handle them.

Tanzania also produces a large number of peaberries which have a much more intense flavor and pungency than the normal beans.

Tanzanian Peaberry

Character: A rich, full flavor with delicate acidity.

Suggested Roast: Medium or dark.

Drinking hints: Can be prepared in all coffee makers. drink with milk or cream for a good all day drinker.

Supplier: H R Higgins was founded in 1942 in a sixth floor attic in London's West End. The company now has premises in Piccadilly where customers can taste as well as buy their teas and coffees.

coffee

Yemen

Simpson & Vail
PO Box 765
3 Quarry Road
Brookfield, CT 06804
USA
Tel: (001) 203 775 0240
Fax: (001) 203 775 0462
e.mail: info@svtea.com

While Ethiopia is thought of as the home of the coffee plant, Yemen (once called Arabia) is said to be the original point from which plants and coffee beans were distributed and transported — the first plant was taken by the Dutch via the port of Mocha in 1616. After their arrival in Yemen in the early 16th century, the Ottamans exported beans to Cairo. In the 18th century, the Yemeni tribespeople were known for preparing their "kahwe" by half roasting and pounding the husks of coffee beans. Fully roasted beans were only used at times of celebration. Today, the coffee drunk in that region is made from half-roasted yellow beans flavored with cardamoms, ginger, cloves, or cinnamon.

Yemeni coffees are known as Mocha and are very small, hard and round, rather irregular in shape and size and yellowy-green in color. Most production areas are very dry, but each has its own microclimate which gives an individual quality and flavor to its coffee. Most are interesting, smooth, and heavy; sometimes fruity, sometimes bitter, sometimes earthy and spicy, sometimes with rich chocolatey tones, which accounts for the fact that the term "mocha" is often used for drinks that mix together chocolate and coffee.

Mocha Yemen Mattari

Character: The Bordeaux of coffees. From the south western tip of the Arabian Peninsula, it has a full body with a dry, winey, chocolatey after taste.

Suggested roast: Medium.

Drinking hints: Ideally suited to brewing in a traditional ibriq in the Turkish or Arabic fashion.

Supplier: Simpson & Vail was founded in 1904 in New York and now provides teas and coffees to many quality restaurants and dining clubs in New York City and to stores across the US and Canada.

After Dinner Blend

Chatz Roasting Company
24963 Huntwood Avenue
Hayward
USA
CA 94544

Fax: (001) 510 265 1734
email: chatzcoffe@aol.com

Like tea, coffee is a beverage that many people enjoy drinking at almost any time of day or night. But in many countries, a small cup of coffee is acknowledged as the perfect sociable ending to an evening dinner as well as a healthy way to help digestion.

From its beginnings in Europe, coffee was thought of as a cure for many ailments. In 1721, Richard Bradley wrote "...it cures consumptions, swooning fits, and the rickets, and that it helps digestion, rarifies the blood, suppresses vapours, gives life and gaiety to the spirits, prevents sleepiness after eating..." Certainly in the 17th, 18th, and 19th centuries, coffee and tea were both healthy drinks simply because they used boiling water (at a time when water was not necessarily a clean or safe commodity) and also offered a sensible alternative to alcohol.

Modern research has shown that coffee does indeed increase the metabolic rate and the breakdown of fat in the body, and some studies suggest that this means that coffee can help in weight loss programmes.

Artamus Blend

Character: A blend of coffees from five major producing areas. Very rich, complex flavor for those who like their coffee dark and strong.

Suggested roast: French roast.

Drinking hints: Brew in a filter or espresso machine. Drinks well without milk, but is also good with milk or cream. An excellent after dinner coffee.

Supplier: Chatz Roasting Company.

coffee

Breakfast Blends

Seattle Coffee Company
5 Rossetti Studios
72 Flood Street
London SW3 5TF
UK
Tel: (00 44) (0)171 495 5531
e.mail:
GarielleShawCommunications@compuserve.com

The blend of coffee that suits most people first thing in the morning or at breakfast time needs to be flavorful and aromatic, not too strong but with enough guts to get you going for the day, bright and smooth, subtle and balanced and that drinks well with milk as a large cappuccino or Fench breakfast style café au lait. Breakfast blends usually contain beans from Africa and Central America.

The addition of milk seems to have developed as a particularly European way of drinking the beverage. In the Arabic countries where coffee originated, milk is not often drunk because the people in those areas have a deficiency of the lactose enzyme needed to digest it. But in Europe, it was common by the end of the 17th century, to add milk to cups of coffee. In 1660, Madame de Sevigné, who commented on both coffee and tea in her diaries, recommended coffee with milk, and by the end of the 18th century, milk was being widely used in coffee in Britain, Germany, Belgium, Switzerland, and Holland.

Mount Rainer Blend

Character: A blend of African and Central American beans. Aromatic and full of flavor, fruity and bright with a smooth long finish.

Suggested roast: Continental roast.

Drinking hints: The perfect breakfast coffee drunk short as an espresso or long with hot milk.

Supplier: Seattle Coffee Company was taken over by Starbucks, the US coffee company in 1998 and the company has over 1,700 shops worldwide.

Decaffeinated

Monmouth Coffee Company
27 Monmouth Street
London WC2H 9DD, UK
Tel: (00 44) (0)171 836 5272
Fax: (00 44) (0)171 379 3801

Caffeine, a natural ingredient that is found in plants such as tea, cocoa, and cola nuts, is just one of the constituents of coffee. It is a mild stimulant that acts on the central nervous system to help increase concentration and alertness. It is absorbed rapidly into the blood and body tissues and it takes about four hours for the concentration of caffeine in the body to decrease by half.

Weight for weight, tea contains more caffeine than coffee, but cup for cup, tea contains less, depending on the type of coffee, the amount used, and the size of the cup.

Most people will not suffer from any negative affects of caffeine consumption if two or three cups a day are drunk. However, some people either do not like the idea of taking in concentrations of caffeine or, for health reasons, cannot. So decaffeinated coffee is the answer.

The first decaffeination process was invented in 1905 in Germany using solvents. The favorite modern method is the "water process" which was perfected in the 1980s.

Colombian Medellin Excelso Decaffeinated

Character: Water processed beans from one of Colombia's best producing regions retains its full bodied flavor and aroma.

Suggested roast: A dark roast gives a strong coffee. Medium roast gives a full bodied, lightly acidic cup. A mix of medium and dark gives a rich full flavor.

Drinking hints: A dark roast makes a perfect strong breakfast or after dinner brew; medium roast or a mixture gives an all day cup.

Supplier: Monmouth Coffee Company was one of London's established and respected coffee stores long before the recent boom in coffee bars and coffee stores made more people in Britain aware of fine coffees.

82

coffee

Espresso Blend

Lavazza Coffee (UK) Ltd
4 Dukes Gate
Acton Lane
Chiswick
London W4 5DX
UK
Tel: (00 44) (0)181 994 6382
Fax: (00 44) (0)181 994 7871

In 1878, the German inventor Gustav Kessel was the first to register a patent for a machine that brewed coffee by forcing water and steam through coffee grounds contained in a filter. But credit is usually given to Italians Luigi Bezzera and Desiderio Pavoni for designing the first real espresso machine. There are certain steps that every good barista will always go through when brewing an espresso — clean the basket in which the grounds sit, check the water pressure, grind the coffee fresh for each cup, measure and tamp down the coffee carefully, watch the machine as the liquid starts to flow, and switch off at the appropriate moment. But all of this is wasted energy if the coffee itself is not up to standard or is not suitable for making espresso.

There is no one particular blend that is the best for making espresso but most blenders recommend medium to high roast beans and, because brewing in this way concentrates the flavor, a coffee that is not too intense in flavor.

Lavazza Qualità Rosso

Character: Traditional, robust blend of *arabica* and *robusta*.

Drinking hints: Although this roast and ground coffee can be brewed in a filter or plunger pot, it is best suited to an espresso machine.

Supplier: Lavazza was founded in Italy by Luigi Lavazza in 1895. Today the company also has offices in the UK, France, Germany, the US, and Vienna.

FairTrade Coffee

Simon Lévelt b.v
KA Hofmanweg 3
2031 BH Haarlem
HOLLAND
Tel: (00 31) 23 512214
Fax: (00 31) 23 5122505

The concept of fairtrade labelling was developed in the Netherlands at the end of 1988 and to date there are seven fairtrade labels in 13 countries.

The idea underpinning fairtrade products is that the workers who grow and produce crops such as sugar, tea, and coffee receive more of the profits direct from the purchaser than they normally would. Agreements are set up and controlled by official fairtrade organizations to make sure that disadvantaged producer groups get a fair price for their product and that they invest a premium amount of their profits into schemes that benefit the workers. Some workers in such places as India, Sri Lanka, Africa, and Latin America are today enjoying improved housing, pension schemes, training facilities, improved medical facilities, etc. Schemes are closely monitored by the official fairtrade bodies to check that the money is used as agreed.

Fairtrade goods are clearly labeled by one or other of the controlling organisations. So that consumers do not become confused, care is taken to ensure that in any one country, only one label is used. In 1996, approximately $150 million (in retail terms) was traded under fairtrade labeling.

Café Beneficio Arabica

Character: A full-bodied, fragrant, and aromatic 100% arabica coffee.

Suggested roast: Medium to dark.

Drinking hints: Brew as espresso or in a cafatière or filter.

Supplier: Simon Lévelt has been an independent family owned company for five generations since 1817 and today has 12 shops in the Netherlands.

coffee

Flavored Coffees

Boaters Coffee Company Ltd
The Coffee Factory
Ampthill
Bedfordshire MK45 2QW
UK
Tel: (00 44) (0)1525 404781
Fax: (00 44) (0)1525 404981

Flavored coffees have been popular in the US for a number of years, and flavoring companies have been developing an increasing range of essential oil, fragrances, and specialty flavors since the mid 1970s. The mid 80s saw the beginning of a growing interest in Britain and other parts of Europe, and now many coffee drinkers enjoy flavored varieties in addition to their usual everyday coffee. The idea appeals particularly to the younger market and packaging is often trendy, bright, and fun, or extremely sophisticated.

With the wider use of cafetières today, catering outlets can offer a range of flavored blends as well as standard coffees as each customer is able to order an individual jug of their chosen brew. Companies creating flavored coffees listen very carefully to their customers and are constantly trying new ideas. All time favorites include double chocolate truffle, tiramisu, sticky toffee, amaretto, Irish whisky cream, rich hazelnut, and exotic liqueur-flavored beans laced with rum, brandy, drambuie, and armagnac.

Amaretto di Saschira

Character: Smooth Colombian coffee with a rich, enticing flavor of the popular Italian liqueur Amaretto de Saschira.

Roast: Medium roast.

Drinking hints: Ideal for cafetières and filter machines. This coffee is great black, but will take a little milk and sugar.

Supplier: Boaters Coffee Company first came across flavored coffees in the US and introduced the idea into the UK in the early 1990s. They now sell more than 150 tons (150,000kg) a year of flavored beans and ground coffees to customers in the UK and Europe.

House Specialties

Algerian Coffee Stores Ltd
52 Old Compton Street
London W1V 6PB
UK
Tel: (00 44) (0)171 437 2480
Fax: (00 44) (0)171 437 5470

Most coffee roasting companies create a variety of house specialties which customers will come back for again and again. Most companies carry a breakfast blend, a rich after dinner blend, an espresso blend, and other more unusual mixtures, depending on their customers' tastes and preferences.

Before a blend can be made up, the blender must have some idea of what he or she is aiming for in terms of flavor, aroma, body, strength, acidity, and price. It is really a question of trial and error. Different coffees are tasted and assessed for those individual characteristics. The possible ingredients for a particular blend are then mixed in different proportions and different roast colors, and each mixture is carefully brewed and tasted and evaluated again to see which balance gives the required character.

There are certain coffee qualities that are known for their blending suitability. For example, *robustas* give body and flavor. A medium roast gives better flavor than a very dark roast. A little Kenya adds acidity. More mature beans from, for example, Sumatra, make for a good after dinner blend. An espresso blend needs the mildness and sweetness of Brazilian Santos and Colombian beans.

Lebanese with Cardamoms

Character: A blend of *arabica* beans that have been roasted and mixed with ground cardamoms. Full bodied, smooth, and spicy.

Suggested roast: High roast.

Drinking hints: Most suitable for a fine grind and brewing in the traditional Arabic or Turkish way with sugar.

Supplier: Algerian Coffee Stores Ltd. has been a landmark in London's Soho for many years. Its teas and coffees are sold by mail order to a worldwide clientele.

Staff at Algerian Coffee Stores are happy to mix the spice with the beans as above, or the two can be provided separately and the customer can blend themselves to suit personal tastes.

Organic Coffee

Paulig UK Ltd
Windsor House
37 Windsor Street
Chertsey
Surrey KT16 8AT
UK
Tel: (00 44) (0)1932 575600
Fax: (00 44) (0)1932 575699

As with so many products today, there is a growing interest amongst the consuming public in organically grown crops. This stems from both concerns for health and also for the long term welfare of our planet. There are a few places around the world where coffee is produced from trees that grow almost wild (in Guatemala for example) and no artificial fertilizers or pesticides are used, so producing a crop that is naturally organic. But chemical pesticides and fertilizers have been in use for a number of years in the coffee industry because of the threat to the plants from disease and bug attacks. Some coffees, such as the Costa Rican Tarrazu, are cultivated without chemical pesticides or herbicides, but are treated with chemical fertilizers to keep the soil rich and healthy.

For a product to be certified "organic" takes several years of patient, labor-intensive work where nature is harnessed to control disease and pests, and natural waste, such as coffee bean husks and shells, are used as compost. Dense planting of trees creates natural shade and also means that there is little need for artificial weed control.

Because of the labor-intensive nature of organic farming, products are often more expensive. But more and more people seem to be taking the attitude that cost is not always the prime consideration.

Ashby's Organic Blend

Character: A vibrant every day roast and ground coffee.

Drinking recommendations: Paulig market this roast coffee ready ground for brewing in filter machines or cafetières. Drink with or without milk.

Supplier: Paulig UK Ltd. is part of the Finnish company which today owns coffee companies including Lyons, Melitta, and Ashbys.

coffee

Coffee Producing Countries

Angola
Australia
Bolivia
Burundi
Cameroon
China
Cuba
Dominican Republic
Ecuador
El Salvador
Galapagos Islands
Guadeloupe

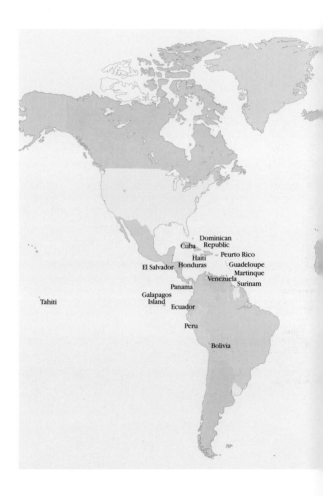

coffees from around the world

Haiti	St Helena
Honduras	Sudan
Ivory Coast	Surinam
Le Réunion	Tahiti
Madagascar	Taiwan
Martinique	Uganda
Mozambique	Venezuela
Panama	Vietnam
Peru	Zaire
Peurto Rico	Zambia
Philippines	Zimbabwe
South Afrcia	

coffee

Acknowledgments

All photographs in this book, unless listed below, were taken by Simon Clay. The publisher would like to thank the following persons and organisations for supplying photography:

Pages 7 (top), 9 (bottom), 11 (top), 13 (middle), 35 (top); The Hulton Getty Picture Collection
Page 7 (middle); Gleason's Pictorial Drawing Room Companion/Corbis
Pages 7 (bottom), 9 (top), 11 (bottom), 13 (top, bottom), 17 (top, middle), 19 (top, bottom), 21 (top, middle) 23 (bottom), 27 (top, middle), 29 (bottom), 31 (top), 35 (bottom), 37 (top); International Coffee Organisation, 22 Berners Street, London W1P 4BD
Page 17 (bottom); Life File/Richard Powers
Page 23 (top); Corbis/Gavin Wickham; Eye Ubiquitous
Page 44 - 45 Life File/Emma Lee

The publisher gratefully acknowledges the generosity of all the suppliers who contributed coffee samples for this book.

Every effort has been made to trace the ownership of all copyrighted material and to secure permission from copyright holders. In the event of any question arising as to the use of any material, we will be pleased to make necessary corrections in future printings.